ALPHA BOOKS

RAINFORESTS

NICOLA BARBER

Evans

EVANS BROTHERS LIMITED

This book is based on **Ecology Watch** RAINFORESTS by Rodney Aldis, first published by Evans Brothers Limited in 1991, but the original text has been simplified.

Evans Brothers Limited
2A Portman Mansions
Chiltern Street
London W1M 1LE

First published 1993

Typeset by Fleetlines Typesetters, Southend-on-Sea
Printed in Spain by GRAFO, S.A. – Bilbao

ISBN 0 237 51324 2

Acknowledgements

Editor: Su Swallow
Language Adviser: Suzanne Tiburtius
Design: Neil Sayer
Production: Jenny Mulvanny

Illustrations: David Gardner, Graeme Chambers
Maps and diagrams: Hardlines, Charlbury

For permission to reproduce copyright material the author and publishers gratefully acknowledge the following:

Cover Eric Crichton, Bruce Coleman Limited
Title page (eyelash viper) Michael Fogden, Oxford Scientific Films
p4 Dr Morley Read, Science Photo Library **p5** (top) Michael Fogden, Oxford Scientific Films, (bottom) Alain Compost, Bruce Coleman Limited **p7** Wardene Weisser, Ardea London Ltd, (inset) M P L Fogden, Bruce Coleman Limited **p8** Dr Morley Read, Science Photo Library **p9** ECOSCENE **p10** Paul Franklin, Oxford Scientific Films **p11** Mark Edwards, Still Pictures **p12** Alain Compost, Bruce Coleman Limited **p13** Kjell B Sanved, Oxford Scientific Films **p14** C McDougal, Ardea London Ltd **p15** Marion Morrison, South American Pictures, (inset) Michael Fogden, Oxford Scientific Films **p16** A G (Bert) Wells, Oxford Scientific Films **p17** Eric Crichton, Bruce Coleman Limited **p18** Wardene Weisser, Ardea London Ltd **p19**
Andy Purcell, Bruce Coleman Limited **p20** (top) Treat Davidson, Frank Lane Picture Agency, (bottom) Phil Devries, Oxford Scientific Films **p21** J Cowan, Bruce Coleman Limited **p22** (top) Hans and Judy Beste, Oxford Scientific Films, (bottom) M P L Fogden, Oxford Scientific Films **p23** François Gohier, Ardea London Ltd **p24** Roberto Bunge, Ardea London Ltd **p25** P Morris, Ardea London Ltd **p26** Jeff Foott, Bruce Coleman Limited **p27** Andrew Plumptre, Oxford Scientific Films **p28** (top) M P L Fogden, Bruce Coleman Limited, (bottom) M P L Fogden, Bruce Coleman Limited **p29** (top) Starin, Ardea London Limited, (bottom) Michael Fogden, Oxford Scientific Films **p30** Michael Fogden, Oxford Scientific Films **p31** Carol Huges, Bruce Coleman Limited **p32** R A Acharya, Dinodia Picture Agency/Oxford Scientific Films **p33** (left) Peter Steyn, Ardea London Ltd, (right) M P L Fogden, Bruce Coleman Limited **p34** (top) Gryniewicz/ ECOSCENE, (bottom) Michael Fogden, Oxford Scientific Films **p35** Philip Sharpe, Oxford Scientific Films **p36** C S Perkins, Magnum Photos **p37** J Hartley, Panos Pictures **p38** Michael K Nichols, Magnum Photos **p39** Marcos Santilli, Panos Pictures **p40** (left) John Mason, Ardea London Ltd, (right) Mark Edwards, Still Pictures **p41** ECOSCENE **p43** (top) Stephen Krasemann, Bruce Coleman Limited, (bottom left) ECOSCENE, (bottom right) Heather Angel **p44** Michael Fogden, Oxford Scientific Films

Contents

Introduction

△ A rainforest in Ecuador

If you look at the map you will see two dotted lines marked Tropic of Capricorn and Tropic of Cancer. Many places between these lines have a hot, wet **climate** and this is where tropical rainforests grow. The largest rainforest is in the Amazon in South America. The Amazon rainforest is bigger than all the other rainforests in the world put together. Southeast Asia, Central and West Africa, Australia and Papua New Guinea also have areas of rainforest.

The tropical rainforests contain a lot of different plants and animals. But every year people cut down or burn more of the rainforests. Many plants and animals die as a result.

TROPICAL RAINFORESTS

Past tropical limit

NORTH AMERICA

Tropic of Cancer

PACIFIC

CENTRAL AMERICA

ATLANTIC OCEAN

Equator

OCEAN

PERU

Amazon BRAZIL

Tropic of Capricorn

SOUTH AMERICA

Past tropical limit

EUROPE

ASIA

SOUTH EAST ASIA

PACIFIC

AFRICA

INDIA

Congo

OCEAN

INDIAN OCEAN

MALAYSIA

INDONESIA

NEW GUINEA

AUSTRALIA

SOUTHERN OCEAN

ANTARCTICA

Tropical evergreen forests

Other tropical rainforests (mostly deciduous)

– – – At different times in the past, tropical rainforests grew much further north and south, and reached these limits.

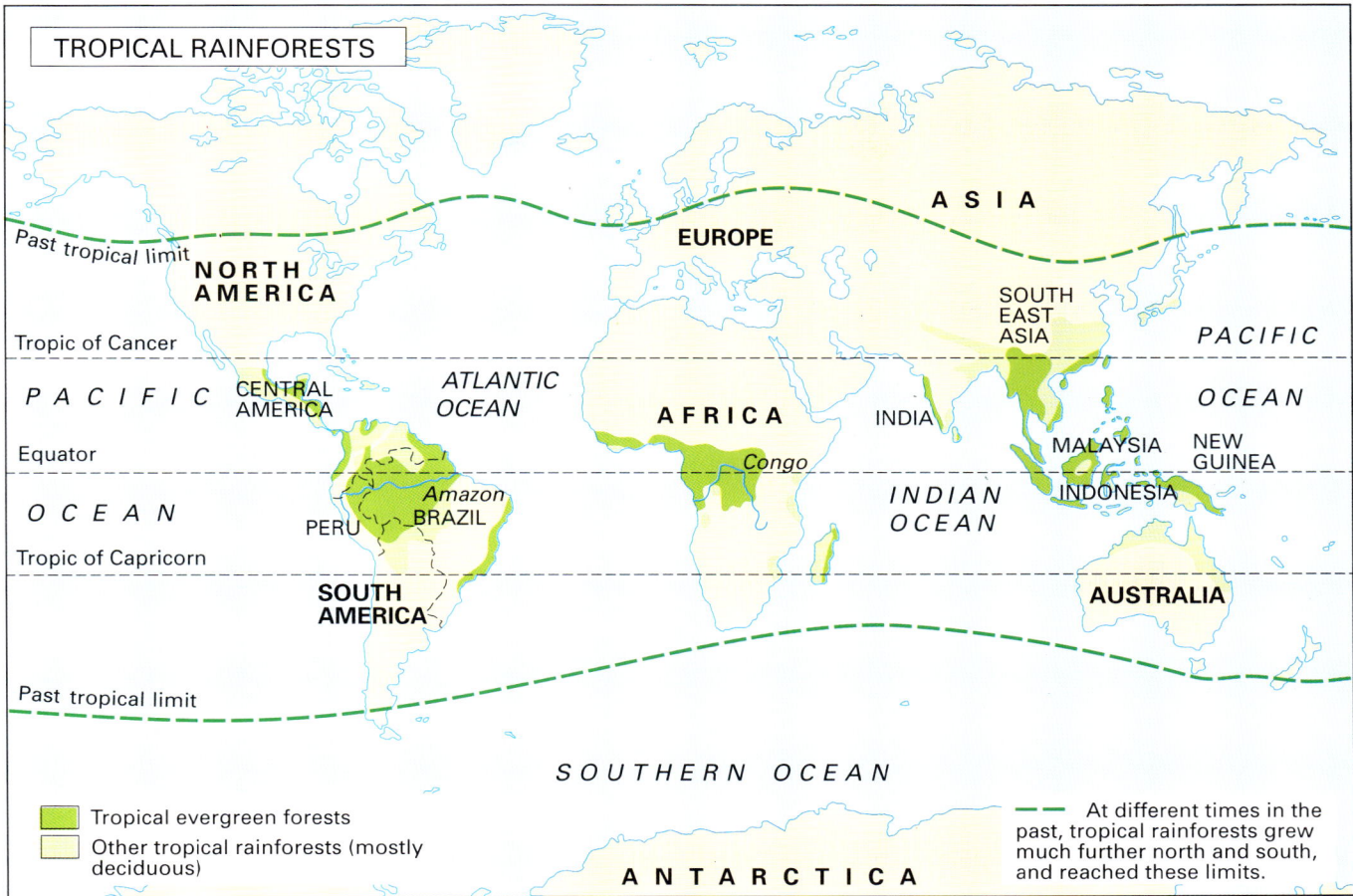

▽ Rainforest wildlife: a lantern bug (below) and a rafflesia flower (bottom)

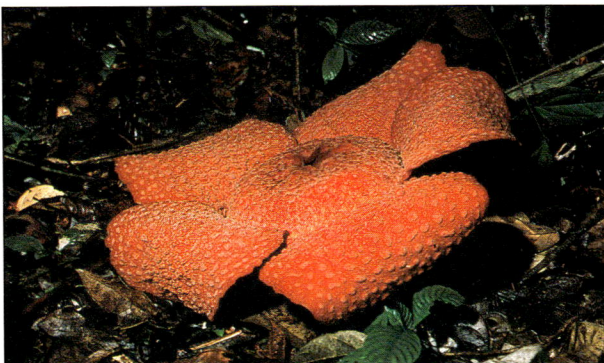

Many tribespeople live in the rainforests. They have learned how to live in the rainforests without damaging them. They use plants and animals from the rainforest for food and medicine. If the rainforests are burned or cut down the forest people find it difficult to keep on living in this way.

climate   The weather conditions in a place over a long time.

5

Sunshine and storms

The climate near the **equator** is warm and wet all year round. In this climate, rainforest trees can grow all the time. They keep their leaves all year. These trees are called evergreen trees. Farther away from the equator there are wet seasons and dry seasons. In the dry seasons, the leaves fall off the trees. Trees that lose their leaves are called deciduous trees.

Rainforest soils

Many plants grow in the rainforests. But the soil in the rainforests does not contain much food for the plants. This is because most tropical soils are very old. All rainforests also have a lot of rain. The rainwater runs through the soil and washes a lot of the food in the soil away. This makes rainforest soil poor and **infertile**.

Rainforest trees can grow in the infertile soil. This is because they also get food from the air and from the rain. Rainforest trees store food in their wood. There is not much food stored in the soil. If people cut the trees down they destroy the stores of food in the rainforest.

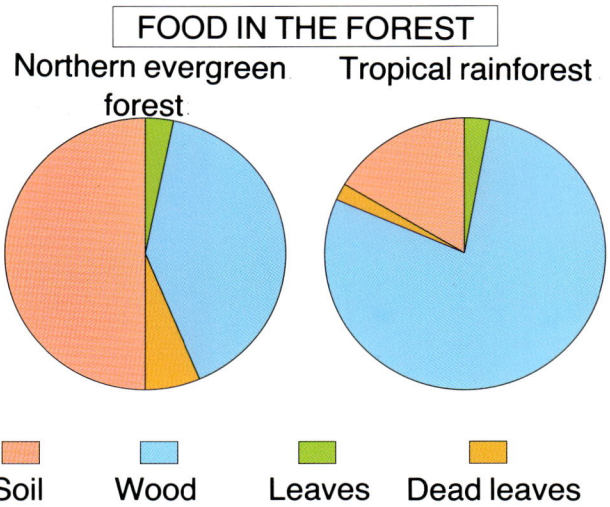

FOOD IN THE FOREST

Northern evergreen forest   Tropical rainforest

Soil   Wood   Leaves   Dead leaves

△ These charts show where plant food is stored in two different kinds of forest.

▷ Rainforests grow in warm, wet climates. (Inset) Fungi live on the leaves that fall to the forest floor.

6

The history of the rainforest

We need to look after the rainforests of the world. To do this, it is important to know about the history of the rainforests.

Some scientists think that many years ago the climate in the tropics was not so wet as it is now. In these dry periods, the rainforests could only grow in a few places. The places where the rainforests grew are called refuges. These refuges may be the oldest parts of the rainforests and we must try to save them from cutting and burning.

Other scientists think that there were floods in the rainforests in the past. For example, the Amazon rainforest was once a huge lake with many islands in it. Different plants and animals developed in the rainforest on each island. When the level of the water went down the plants and animals could move out into the new rainforest. This is why there are so many different kinds of plants and animals living in the rainforests today.

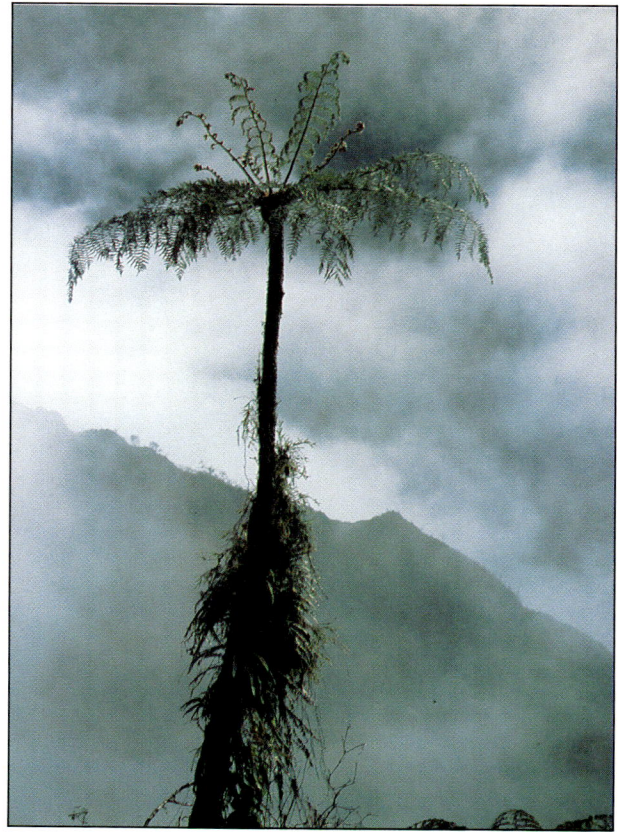

△ A rainforest tree high in the Andes Mountains

REFUGES

This map shows the places where rainforests grew in South America when the climate was drier.

△ A rainforest river

Why rainforests are important

Rainforests are important for many reasons. If heavy rain falls directly on to the ground it can quickly wash away the soil. This is called erosion. Rainforests help to stop erosion. This is because the rainwater falls on to the trees first, before it drops to the ground. The leaves on the trees slow the raindrops down.

Rainforests also help to stop flooding. After heavy rain the rainforest trees soak up some of the water. This stops all the rainwater running into streams and rivers at the same time.

Floods in Bangladesh

In Bangladesh floods often cover huge areas of land. The River Ganges runs from the Himalayan Mountains through Bangladesh to the Indian Ocean. Forest once covered the sides of the Himalayan Mountains. But people have cut down much of this forest. When heavy rain falls there are no trees to soak up the rainwater, so it runs quickly into the River Ganges. This makes the river flood. Many thousands of people lose their homes. Their fields are covered with water, and their crops are destroyed.

Spreading the heat

Rainforests also help to keep the world's weather from getting too hot. Heat from the rainforest is stored in water **vapour**. The water vapour rises into the air above the rainforest. About ten kilometres above earth the water vapour changes into water droplets. The heat moves into the air around the vapour. The warm air then moves towards cooler parts of the world. This means that the heat of the rainforests helps to warm some colder parts of the world. If people cut down too many rainforests it could change the world's weather.

▽ Heavy rain falls almost every day in the rainforests.

◁ Rainwater soon washes away bare soil.

The 'greenhouse effect'

People burn down rainforests to clear the land for crops. But this affects the world's weather too. Some gases in the air around the earth trap heat. The heat warms the earth. But if there are too many of these gases in the air, they trap too much heat. This is called the 'greenhouse effect' because heat can get into a greenhouse through the glass, but it cannot get out again. One of the gases in the air is called carbon dioxide. Plants use carbon dioxide to make food. So the trees in the rainforest have carbon dioxide in their leaves. When people burn the trees the carbon dioxide moves back into the air. The carbon dioxide traps more heat around the earth. Some scientists think that about one quarter of carbon dixoide being released into the air comes from burning rainforests.

If the greenhouse effect gets worse the earth will warm up. The ice caps at the North and South poles might melt. There would be more water in the oceans. This would cause floods and many people would lose their homes and their land.

equator The imaginary line around the middle of the earth, half way between the North and South poles.
infertile soil Soil where plants cannot grow well.
vapour Tiny drops of water in the air.

11

The rainforest layers

The rainforest is made up of several layers of plants. The top three layers are tree layers. Below them is a layer of shrubs and young trees. Under that is the forest floor.

In the evergreen forests the trees have leaves all year round. The leaves stop light from reaching the lower layers. Not many bushes and plants can grow there. But in the deciduous rainforests the trees lose their leaves. Light can reach the lower layers for part of the year. In these forests there is a thick layer of bushes.

▽ The giant flying squirrel lives in the tree tops.

Top tree layer

Forest canopy

Lower canopy

△ Flowers such as this bromeliad grow in the rainforest canopy.

Up in the roof

The tops of the taller trees form the middle tree layer. This is called the forest canopy. The canopy is the roof of the forest. It stops light from reaching the forest floor. The canopy also stops water from escaping out of the forest. This makes the rainforest a dark, warm and damp place. Many rainforest animals live in the canopy. The giant flying squirrel can glide from one tree top to another.

◁ The layers of the rainforest

Shrub layer

Above and below

Some very tall trees grow above the forest canopy. This is the top tree layer. Large birds use these trees to make their nests. Some smaller trees live beneath the forest canopy. This is the bottom tree layer. It is called the lower canopy. Palm trees like the damp air and dim light in the lower canopy. Many birds live there. They feed on insects.

The bottom layers

The shrub layer is below the lower canopy. It is even darker than the lower canopy. Usually, not many plants can grow in the shrub layer. But sometimes trees fall over or die and this leaves a hole in the forest canopy. Light gets down to the shrub layer and plants begin to grow. Many animals eat the shrub plants. Deer, buffaloes and tapir eat young leaves. Orang utans and gorillas also live in the shrub layer.

Below the shrub layer is the forest floor. The floor is covered with dead leaves and rotting wood. Small animals such as termites live on the forest floor. Fungi grow on the dead leaves and wood.

▷ Underneath the forest canopy the rainforest is dark. (Inset) Leaf frogs live in the wet, warm rainforest.

▽ Orang utans live in the shrub layers of the rainforests of Asia.

14

Life in the rainforest

Millions of different kinds of animals and plants live in the rainforests. Each one has a job to do in the life of the rainforest. One of the main jobs for insects and birds is to carry **pollen**. Pollen comes from flowers. When an insect or bird carries pollen from one flower to another of the same type it is called pollination. After pollination the flower can produce a seed. The seed may grow into a new plant. Birds, bats, bees and hawk moths all carry pollen.

▷ The brightly coloured passion flower attracts birds.

▽ A hawk moth

In the middle of the flower is a sweet liquid called nectar. Nectar is a rich food for birds, bats and insects. As they drink the nectar, pollen rubs on to them. When they visit another plant for more nectar, the pollen rubs off again.

Flower attraction

Flowers attract birds, bats and insects in various ways. Bright colours like red attract birds. Yellow and blue flowers with a weak scent attract bees. Flowers with a strong scent attract moths and bats. Many moths and bats only come out at night. The strong scent helps them to find the flowers.

▽ Hummingbirds have long, curved beaks.

△ Butterflies have long tongues to reach the nectar inside a flower.

Many flowers are made so that only certain animals can reach their nectar. Hummingbirds have long, curved beaks. They go to flowers which have a long, tube shape. Their beaks fit into the tube-shaped flower to reach the nectar at the end. Parkias are also rainforest plants. They are visited by bats. Parkias have flowers on long stalks. The flowers hang down below the forest canopy. Bats can reach the flowers without damaging their wings.

Butterflies and moths have long tongues. They reach deep inside flowers with their long tongues.

Butterflies are very light so they can stand on the flowers while they drink the nectar. But moths are heavier than butterflies. This means that moths cannot stand on the flowers. Instead, a moth hovers in the air by a flower while it drinks.

Helping each other

Some plants and animals work together to help one another survive. The brazil nut tree, the orchid plant and the orchid bee are like this. This is how it works. The brazil nut tree grows in the rainforest. The orchid plant grows on the brazil nut tree in the forest canopy. The orchid plant attracts male orchid bees, and they carry the pollen of the orchid plant from flower to flower. The brazil nut tree also has flowers, and these flowers attract female orchid bees. Only big, strong bees like the orchid bee are able to push back the tough covering of the brazil nut flowers. The female orchid bees then carry the pollen of the brazil nut tree from flower to flower. In this way,

△ A humming hawk moth hovers by a flower.

▽ An orchid bee and an orchid plant

20

the brazil nut tree, the orchid plant and the orchid bee help one another to live. If one of them died out, the others would not survive.

▽ There are many different kinds of orchid in the rainforests.

pollen   Fine powder produced by plants. Each tiny grain of pollen is a male cell that can fertilize other flowers of the same type.

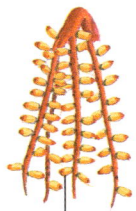

Spreading the seeds

Some animals take pollen from plant to plant. Other animals spread seeds around the rainforest. Some seeds may fall in places where they cannot grow. Other seeds will grow into new plants.

△ A black flying fox bat

◁ Ginger plants grow on the forest floor.

22

△ Squirrel monkeys eat mostly fruit.

Seed spreaders

Plants grow tasty fruit to attract animals. The seeds stick to the fruit. When the animals take the fruit they spread the seeds far from the plant. Large birds such as toucans and hornbills spread seeds around the rainforest. Monkeys and apes like sweet fruits that hang down from branches. They can reach the fruit with their hands.

Bats are also important seed-spreaders. The bats carry the fruit to their **roosting sites**. Then the bats eat the flesh of the fruit. The seeds drop to the ground.

Birds

The toucans of the Central and South American rainforests eat large fruits. Sometimes these fruits have only one seed. The birds eat the fruit and spit the seed out. In Africa and Asia hornbills eat the same kind of fruits.

Another bird that spreads seeds is the pigeon. There are pigeons all over the world. Some pigeons live in cities. Many live in woodlands and grasslands. But some pigeons in Southeast Asia and Australia live in rainforests. In Australia, the red-crowned and wompoo pigeons eat rainforest fruits. Fruits with bright colours attract the pigeons.

Some animals will eat many different kinds of fruits. But the quetzal bird of Central America only eats the fruits of the wild avocado tree. The quetzal bird depends upon the tree for food. The wild avocado tree depends upon the quetzal bird to spread its seeds.

Some birds destroy seeds instead of spreading them. Parrots eat the seed itself instead of the fruit. The macaw parrots of Central and South America destroy seeds. They pull off the fruit with their beaks. Then they crack the seed open and eat it.

△ The macaw parrot has a strong, hard beak for cracking seeds open.

▷ The quetzal eats the fruits of the wild avocado tree.

24

Fruit-eating fish

In many parts of the Amazon rainforest fish eat fruit from the trees. The trees grow on the banks of the rivers and drop their fruits and seeds into the water. The fish eat the fruit and then carry the seeds to another part of the river. Sometimes the river floods. The seeds settle on land and grow into new plants.

▽ Rainforest trees on a river bank

△ A female buffalo with its baby

Elephants and buffaloes

Elephants and buffaloes live in the Asian and African rainforests. They eat the fruits of the rainforest trees. The seeds are spread in the animals' droppings. Elephants and buffaloes can travel a long way in a day. So the seeds are spread far away. Elephants and buffaloes move from the rainforests to the grasslands. Sometimes the animals drop seeds from the rainforest trees in the grasslands and new trees grow up. Hornbills come and sit in their branches. The trees form a new area of rainforest. In this way, elephants and buffaloes help to make more rainforests.

Help from horses

In Central America there are no elephants and buffaloes. But 400 years ago people brought horses from Spain to Central America. The horses now live on farms called ranches. In Costa Rica there are many ranches on the grasslands. But these grasslands used to be rainforests. Now the rainforest is spreading on to the grasslands again. This is because the horses are allowed to live on the grasslands and in the rainforests. They spread seeds from the rainforests on to the grasslands. Slowly, new areas of rainforest are growing up.

roosting sites The places where bats or birds build their nests.

27

Poisonous plants

The seeds and leaves of plants are food for many animals. But plants must also protect their seeds and leaves. If they did not, animals might eat all of the plant and the plant might die out. Plants protect themselves against animals in various ways. Many plants have poisons to stop animals eating their leaves or seeds.

▽ Katydids feed on plants' leaves.

Plants often cover their seeds in poisons. Others have poisonous leaves. Animals must make the poisons harmless before they can eat

▽ Many plants protect their leaves with poisons.

△ Colobus monkeys can eat poisonous leaves quite safely.

the seeds or leaves. Different kinds of plants use different poisons. An animal might be able to make one kind of poison harmless. But the animal is unlikely to be able to make all the poisons harmless. So each kind of plant is only eaten by one or two kinds of animal.

Monkey tricks

Many different animals eat plants. Large animals, such as monkeys, eat a little from lots of different kinds of plants. They swallow small amounts of different poisons. Smaller animals, such as beetles, often feed on only one kind of plant.

Monkeys eat many kinds of seeds and leaves. The Uakaris monkey lives in the Amazon rainforest. It cracks open the hard shells of seeds with its teeth. In the rainforests of Central and South America lives the howler monkey. Howler monkeys live in large groups in the lower canopy of the forest. The leaves are less poisonous in the lower canopy than in the higher forest canopy. The colobus monkey lives in the African rainforests. It has a liquid in its stomach to make leaf poisons harmless.

▽ Some beetles feed on leaves.

Insect eaters

Many insects feed on plants. Insects eat the leaves, pollen and seeds of a plant. There are so many different insects in the rainforests that it is difficult to imagine. Scientists have counted gver 900 different kinds of insect in one rainforest tree. Many insects can make a plant's poison harmless. Sometimes the insect stores the poison from the plant inside its own body. The insect uses the poison to protect itself from larger animals, such as spiders and ladybird beetles.

▷ Caterpillars feed on leaves.

Chemical cures

People can use many of the poisons made by plants. Many medicines are made from plants. But there are many unknown plants in the rainforests. They may be useful to people in the future. We need to protect every plant and animal in the rainforests.

◁ The wood-boring beetle feeds on nectar.

Teeth, claws and more

Most animals eat plants. But some animals eat other animals. They are called **carnivorous** animals. The carnivorous animals are all sizes, from insects, spiders, frogs, snakes and lizards to tigers. When rainforests are cut down and burned many animals die. This means that there is less food for the carnivorous animals. So they die too.

The big cats
Several kinds of wild cat live in the rainforests. In Asia the tiger lives in the rainforests. Tigers can kill and eat buffaloes, deer, antelopes and wild pigs. In Central and South America the rainforests are home to the jaguar. Jaguars can climb high into the forest canopy. They leap from branch to branch chasing sloths and spider monkeys. Jaguars also hunt

▽ The tiger lives in the rainforests of Asia.

△ The bird-eating spider traps hummingbirds and eats them.

◁ Birds of prey such as the crowned eagle nest in the forest canopy.

along rivers for alligators. Both tigers and jaguars need a lot of space to live and hunt.

Birds of prey
Some birds are carnivorous. These birds are called birds of prey. The eagles are birds of prey. There are different kinds of eagle in all the large rainforests. In South America there is the harpy eagle. In Asia lives the monkey-eating eagle. Africa is home to the crowned eagle. These large birds sit on branches high up in the rainforest. They fly down to kill animals in the forest canopy.

Frogs and lizards

Many frogs, snakes and lizards live in the rainforests. They all eat other animals. Frogs eat insects. A frog catches insects with its long tongue. Many frogs live high in the forest canopy. But frogs are eaten by other animals. Herons, egrets and snakes all hunt frogs. Some frogs have poisons in their skin to protect themselves.

△ The chameleon lizard lives in the tree tops.

▽ The arrow poison frog lives in South America. It makes poisons in its skin.

Poisonous frogs are often brightly coloured. This warns other animals not to eat them.

The chameleon lizard also lives in the tree tops. It grips on to branches with its feet tail. It catches insects with its long tongue. The chameleon lizard can change colour. It is usually green and brown. But if another animal attacks it, the chameleon turns bright blue and red.

▷ A parrot snake

Snakes in the forest
Snakes hunt in the forest canopy. They can climb and move about quietly. Some snakes use poison to kill other animals. Some snakes wrap themselves around other animals to strangle them.

carnivorous Describes an animal that eats meat.

Farming the forests

△ The Yanomami people live in the Amazon rainforests.

▷ Farmers burn large areas of the rainforest to make fields.

About 1000 different tribes live in the rainforests of the world. The Yanomami tribe lives in the Amazon in South America. The Baku tribe lives in rainforests in Africa. The Penans tribe lives in Southeast Asia. The people of these tribes have lived in the rainforests for thousands of years. These people have learned how to live in the rainforests without damaging them.

Different tribes have different ways of living in the rainforests. Some hunt animals and gather plants for food. Others grow crops in the rainforests. The people of the tribes know which fruits and nuts are good to eat. They use rainforest plants as medicines. They use poison from plants for hunting and fishing.

Farmers
The Yanomami tribe lives in the Amazon rainforest in South America. The Yanomami people grow crops in the rainforest. They cut down trees to make a small garden. They burn the trees and put the ash on to the soil. The tree ash is full of plant food (see page 6). It makes the soil fertile so that crops will grow.

The Yanomami grow many different crops. They grow maize (sweetcorn), sweet potatoes, cassava, bananas and palms. They grow all the plants mixed together. The tall plants such as the bananas and palms

protect the maize and sweet potatoes from the sun and rain.

After about three years the Yanomami leave their garden. This is because the soil does not have enough goodness left to grow any more crops. The Yanomami cut another garden in a different part of the rainforest. The rainforest trees slowly grow back in the old garden. It takes at least 50 years for the trees to replace the plant food taken by the crops.

In some places, people from outside the rainforests have moved into the forests. They clear the trees to make large fields. They grow their crops in the fields. But after a few years there is no goodness left in the soil. The people have to leave the fields. Then they cut down more rainforest to make new fields.

Rainforests of the future

We must save the rainforests of the world for the future. But the problems are different in different parts of the world. In some places people cut down the rainforest trees for their wood. This is called logging. In some places farmers cut down the rainforest trees. The farmers need land to grow their crops. In other places people burn the rainforest. These people are ranchers. They use the land to graze their cattle. This has happened in the Amazon rainforests. But after only five or six

▽ In the Amazon, the rainforest is burned down to make land for cattle.

years there is no goodness left in the soil (see page 6). No more grass will grow. Then the ranchers must burn more rainforest to make more land for their cattle.

Tropical woods

Logging has caused a lot of damage in the rainforests of South Asia and Africa. In the future, logging could also damage the rainforests in Central and South America. Scientists are looking at ways to take trees from the rainforests without damaging the forests.

Scientists are doing an experiment in Peru in South America. They have cut down trees in the rainforest. But they have cut the trees in narrow strips between 20 metres and 50 metres wide. This means that animals can cross the strips and drop seeds on the way (see page 22). After about three or four years shrubs are already growing back across the strips. After about 30 or 40 years people can cut down the trees in these strips again.

△ Large areas of rainforest are cut down for wood.

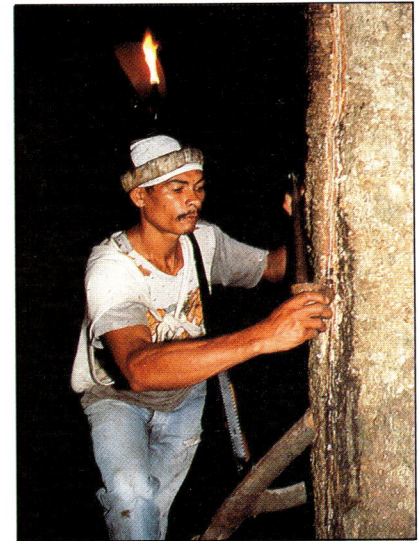

△ Rubber tapping in the rainforest

◁ Farmers plant palm trees for palm oil.

Agroforestry
Sometimes people grow trees and crops together. This is called agroforestry. In tropical countries the trees provide shelter for the soil and the crops. Some farmers grow teak trees amongst their crops. When the teak trees are big enough, the farmers cut them down. The farmers sell the teak wood and the wood is used to make furniture. The farmers then plant new teak trees. Farmers also grow palm trees in agroforestry. The palm trees are used for their palm oil.

In many places ranchers have cleared rainforest land and then left it empty. Agroforestry could be useful in these areas. Farmers could grow their crops and trees on this cleared land. This means that they would not need to cut down more rainforest to grow their crops.

Making a living

Some people make a living from the natural rainforest. For more than 100 years people have collected brazil nuts from brazil nut trees. People have also taken natural rubber from the rubber trees. This is called rubber tapping. These are both ways that people can make a living from the rainforests without damaging them.

▽ In Papua New Guinea the rainforests are being cut down. This threatens the way of life of the tribespeople.

Tribal lands

In many places new farmers, loggers and ranchers are moving into the rainforests. These new people often threaten the way of life of the rainforest tribes. This has happened in Colombia in South America. But the government of Colombia has given the rainforest land to the rainforest tribes. These tribes are called the Yakuna Indians. The government helps the Yakuna Indians to protect the rainforest in Colombia.

National parks

Some governments have set up national parks to protect rainforests. One example is the Korup Park in Cameroon in Africa. The Park is divided into different areas. In the National Park no hunting or logging is allowed. Local people live in other areas of the Park. In these areas, the local people are allowed to fish, hunt animals and collect plants. The Korup Park also protects the area around the River Korup. Mangrove plants grow in the River Korup, and many young fish live there.

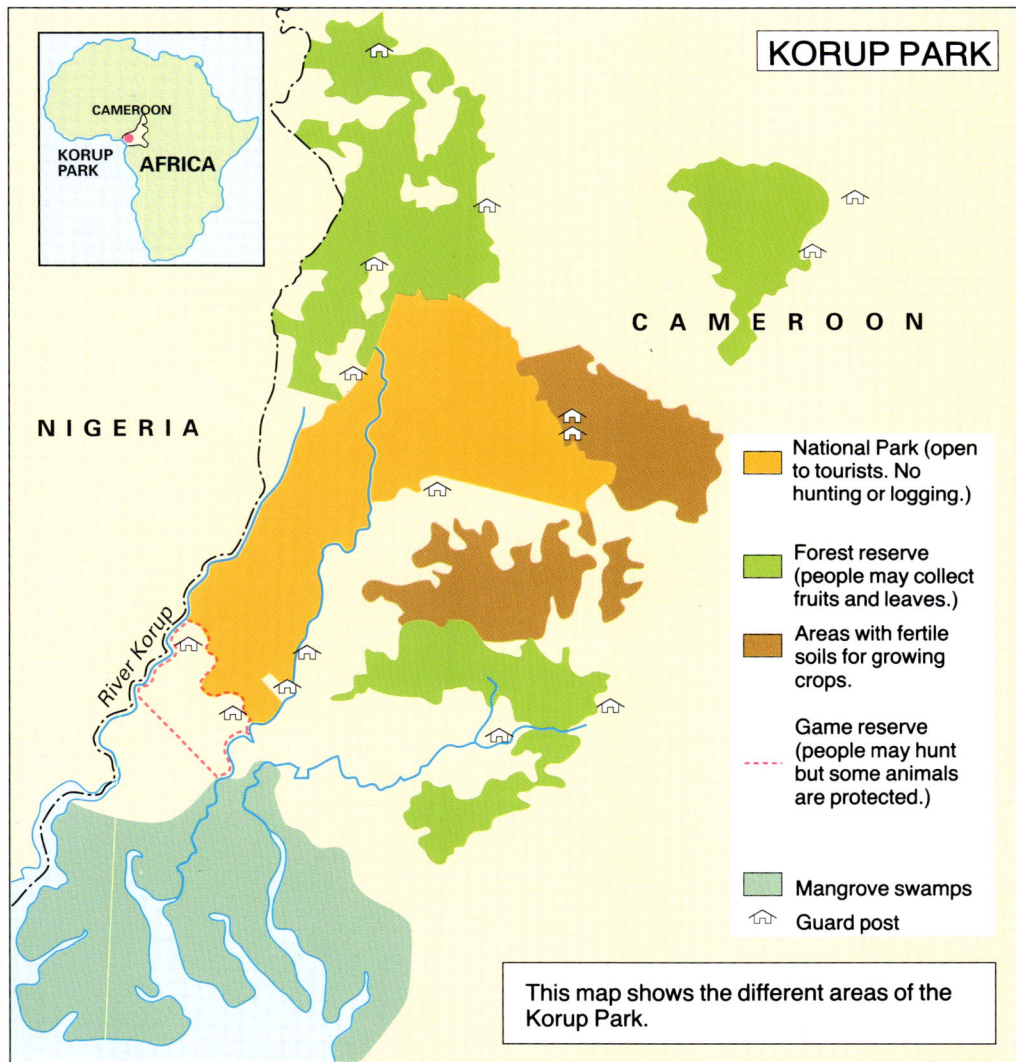

◁ The Korup Park is in Cameroon in West Africa.

KORUP PARK

CAMEROON
KORUP PARK
AFRICA

CAMEROON

NIGERIA

River Korup

National Park (open to tourists. No hunting or logging.)

Forest reserve (people may collect fruits and leaves.)

Areas with fertile soils for growing crops.

Game reserve (people may hunt but some animals are protected.)

Mangrove swamps

⌂ Guard post

This map shows the different areas of the Korup Park.

In Peru

The largest national park in the world is in Peru. It is called the Manu National Park. It lies around the River Manu. So far, scientists have found 1000 different kinds of bird, 13 kinds of monkey, 110 kinds of bat and over 15,000 kinds of plant in the Park. Jaguars also live there. Many tourists visit the Park. This provides jobs for the local people. The government of Peru makes sure that tourists do not harm the animals and plants in the Park.

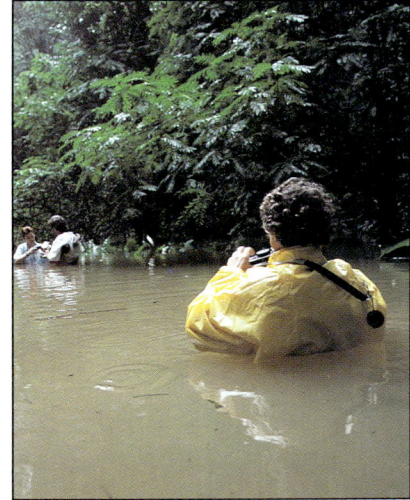

△ Tourists in the water in a rainforest park.

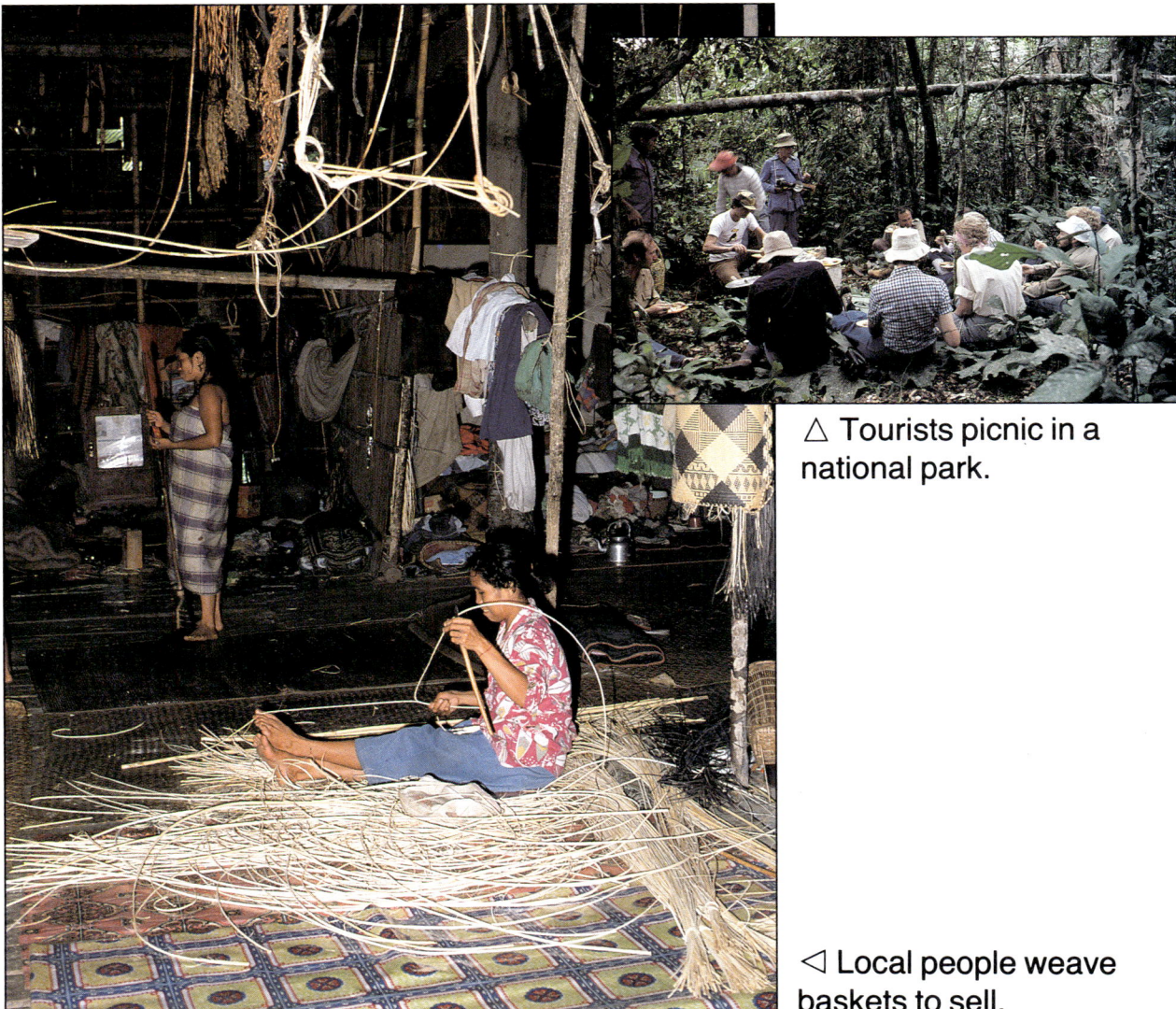

△ Tourists picnic in a national park.

◁ Local people weave baskets to sell.

43

Saving the rainforests

We have seen that many animals and plants live in the rainforests of the world. But the rainforests are home to people too. It is important to protect the rainforests for the future, but we must also think about the people who live in them'. Many rainforests grow in countries where the people are very poor. These people need to earn a living. They would also like to improve the way they live. The rich countries of the world must help the poorer countries to protect the animals and plants of the rainforests. The rich countries must also help the people who live in the rainforests. How this can be done is the main challenge for the future.

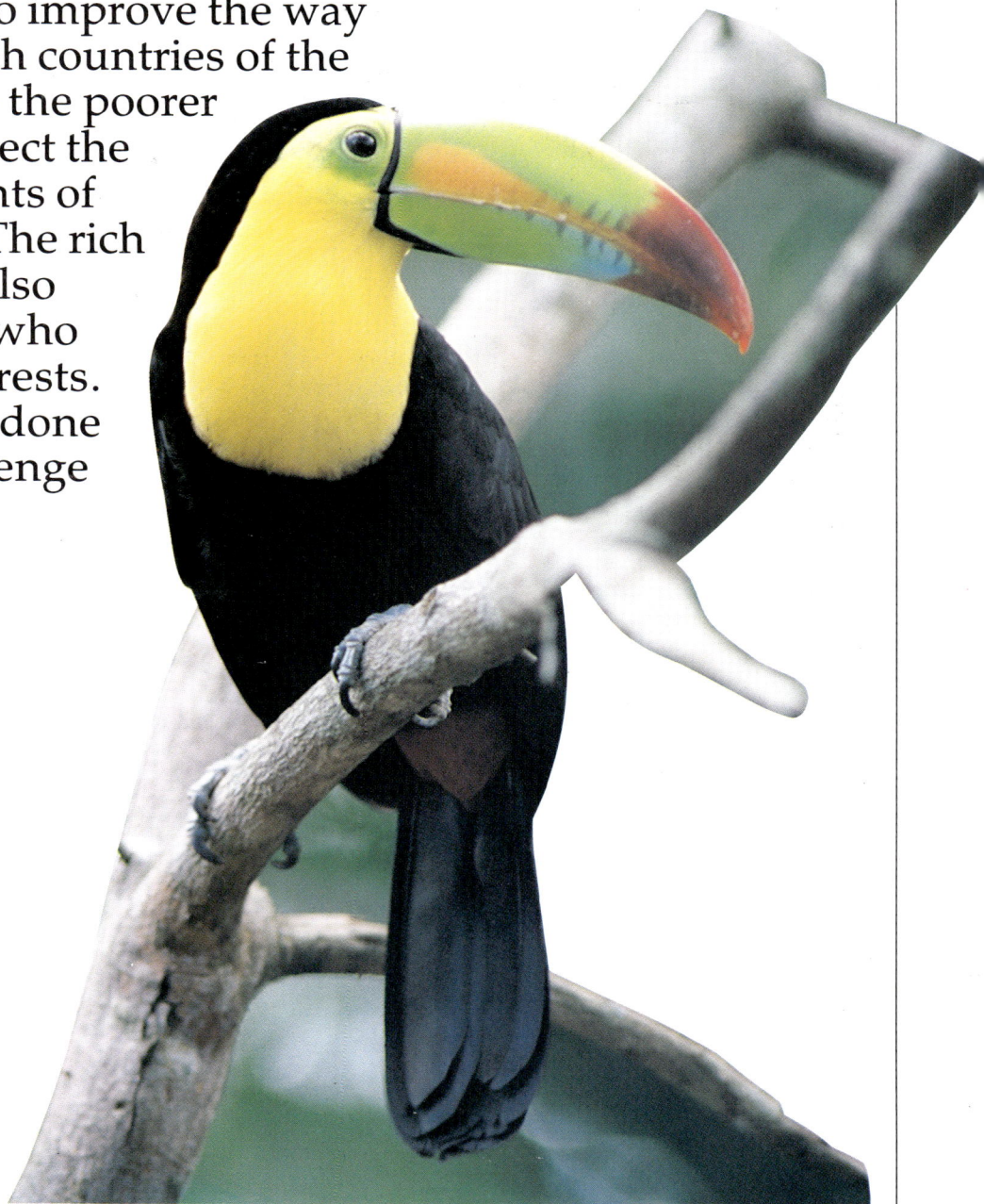

A toucan. Toucans live in the rainforests of Central and South America.